SIAI Marchetti SF-260

Photo: Walter Van Bel

SF-260
Marchetti

Military pilots, no matter if they are fighter pilots, reconnaissance pilots, flying transport aircraft or any other type of aircraft, they all had to learn how to fly. To this purpose, basic training aircraft are developped and built, to be flown by experienced instructors and first time student pilots. One of these is the SIAI Marchetti SF.260, a successful aircraft that was selected by over 30 countries to train their future airmen. The origins of the aircraft go back to 1964, when the prototype, then known as the F.250 - referring to its 250 hp Lycoming engine - was first flown. Soon after, the aircraft went into production, however it was powered with a 260 hp engine, changing the designation of the aircraft to SF.260. Some of the first Air Forces to buy the aircraft, often referred to as Marchetti, were Italy, Belgium and Ireland. I remember seeing them flying with the Belgian Air Force, sporting a very smart dark green and brown camouflage with an impressive shark mouth. Today, the shark mouth is still there, but the overall livery has changed into yellow, red or grey.

The majority of photos in this book were made by editor Robert Pied, who lives just a 5 minute walk from Beauvechain air base, the home of the Belgian Air Force Marchettis. Many of the Italian SF.260s were photographed by Giorgio Chiarini, who also participated in our book on the Eurofighter Typhoon. Many other photographers helped us with photos, we have listed them below. A special mention goes to Rogier Westerhuis, who made some fantastic photos of Philippine and Sri Lankan SF.260 TPs.
We hope you'll enjoy this photographical portrait of the smart and elegant SF.260

Photo: Giorgio Ciarini

Special thanks to these gentlemen, all good-looking: Robert Pied, Giorgio Ciarini, Bart Rosselle, Rogier Westerhuis, Kris Christiaens, Gert Trachez, Walter Van Bel, Laurent Heylighen, Augusto Quincke, Peter Anthoni, Rob Palmer, Rob Schleiffert and Gunter Geens.

Photo: Frank Grealish

Photo: Kris Christiaens

Above: This fantastic photo shows a Marchetti of the Irish Air Corps making a hard lefthand turn over the snowcovered hills of the island. The Irish aircraft were SF-260WE Warriors, equipped with underwing hardpoints. After the arrival of the PC-9, Ireland sold its Marchettis to a private reseller in the US.

Left: Active for over 50 years, the SF-260 is the aircraft on which every Belgian military pilot learned to fly. Easy to maintain, very forgiving and agile; these are some of the advantages of the SIAI-Marchetti 260.

Photo: Via Duke Archives

Left: The Marchetti is mainly used as a training aircraft, but it can also be used as a close air support aircraft. This is an SF-260WL Warrior in the colours of the Burkina Faso Air Force. The Warrior-version of the SF-260 can be equipped with underwing hardpoints to carry light weapons. Notice in this photo the black blade antenna on the vertical tail extension and the white antenna on the belly.
In all, the SIAI Marchetti SF.260 has been sold to the air forces of over 30 countries, from Belgium to Zimbabwe and Burundi to Zambia.

SF-260 Marchetti Types

Although most SF.260s are very similar - with the exception of the TP-version, which has a completely different nose to house turboprop engine and is equipped with a 3-blade propeller - sevral types have been developped. The photo to the right shows one of the initial 33 SF.260AM built for the Italian Air Force. Later, a second batch of 30 aircraft for Italy were constructed, these being SF.260EA. One of the most produced SF.260s is the SF.260ML, built for Libya. Some 240 of this version were built. Some of these aircraft were later sold to Burkina Faso, Burundi, Nicaragua, Uganda and possibly other countries such as Chad. The most evolved version is the SF.260F, which is an upgraded version of the D-model, with a fuel-injected engine. Of these 6 have been sold to Zimbabwe.

Photo: Laurent Heyligen

Photo: Gert Trachez

Above: Sitting in the far left SIAI Marchetti of a 6-ship formation, Gert Trachez captures this great shot near the Belgian Air Force base of Beauvechain. Belgium has two types of the aircraft in service: the SF-260M and the SF-260D. The difference is mostly in the engine; while the M-version is equipped with a Avco Lycoming 0-540-E4-A5 engine, the D-version has an AE10-540-D4A5 engine, which features a servo-operated fuel injection system. Both engine provide the aircraft with 260 hp. There are some differences in the forward instrument panel as well, we'll get to that further in this book!

Photo: Rogier Westerhuis

Left: In 1980, the SF-260TP was developped, a variant of the aircraft, powered by a 350 HP Allison Model 250 turboprop engine. To house the larger engine, the nose of the aircraft had to be re-designed and the aircraft got fitted with a larger 3-blade propeller. This photo shows a SF-260TP in service with the Philippine Air Force, which has 18 of it in service, next to the M, W and FH-versions. Other countries that operate the turboprop version are Burundi, Ethiopia and Zambia. Haiti, Sri Lanka and the UAE used to fly the type as well, but have retired them recently.

Photo: Kris Christiaens

Photo: Robert Pied

Photo: Duke Archives

Top: ST-31, an updated SF.260M of the Belgian Air Force and one of the "Red Devils" Demonstration Team is retracting it's landing gear, moments after take off. Above: The aircraft's spinner, having been removed. Left: The two-bladed Hartzell propellor.

The SIAI Marchetti SF.260 is a propellor driven training aircraft which is powered by an Avco Lycoming engine with six cylinders in line. The front part of the aircraft has two large openings on either side of the spinner, providing the engine with air. Below the spinner, the SF.260s landing light is located. Notice the radiator located underneath the fuselage.
The SIAI Marchetti SF.260 is an all-metal training aircraft that has been in service with the Belgian Air Force for over 50 years.

Photo: Jean-Paul Vingerhoed

Photo: Robert Pied

Photo: Robert Pied

Photo: Robert Pied

These two photos show the openings in the nose of the aircraft and the differences between the port and starboard one. Notice the chipping.

Photo: Robert Pied

Photo: Robert Pied

Above: Immediately below the spinner, a landing light is located. Below: this black-and-grey Italian SF-260 EA is taxiing back from the runway, with its landing light on. Notice the lowered trailing edge flaps, the darkened centre section of the canopy and the wing fences on the leading edge of the wings, typical for this subtype.

Photo: Giorgio Ciarini

Photo: Giorgio Giarini

Above: A technician is checking the cockpit of this Italian SF.260 EA. The EA-version is the latest version of the aircraft and some 30 of them were built, exclusively for the Italian Air Force. Notice the different panels on the aft fuselage, compared to the Belgian M or D-versions. Notice the nose art painted on the engine cover, which is in close-up in the photo to the right.

Photo: Laurent Heyligen

The SIAI Marchetti SF.260 was a much more modern aircraft when compared to the training aircraft that were used earlier. In the case of the Belgian Air Force, student pilots used to be trained on SV.4 biplanes, T-6 harvards and later on in their training on the Fouga Magister jet trainer. In order to obtain their "wings", students have to complete 125 flying hours, which include flight training, instrument flying, formation flying, night flying, navigation and aerobatics. Of these 125 hours, 41 hours are done solo.

Photo: Robert Pied

Photo: Robert Pied

The nose of the aircraft in closer detail. In all, it comprises of 4 engine panels, all of which can be easily removed, and the front engine part with the spinner. The white part in the photo above is the GPS antenna. In the initial M-version, this used to be underneath the canopy, aft of the backseats.

Photo: Robert Pied

Photo: Robert Pied

Above: On the starboard side of the nose, an earthing point is located. Notice the structure of the wing root. Right: The port side of the nose of the SF.260. Belgium initially bought 36 SF.260M aircraft, but placed a second order for 9 aircraft to replace some of the aircraft that were lost in crashes. The new aircraft arrived in 1992 and were SF.260D aircraft, which had a slightly more powerful engine, newer cockpit and larger canopy.

Photo: Robert Pied

Photo: Robert Pied

Photo: Robert Pied

Left: The Marchetti's engine uses ordinary petrol and these are the engine exhausts, located underneath the nose, near the nose landing gear.

Photo: Robert Pied

Left: A view of the forward fuselage, seen from above. Notice the smaller air intakes near the base of the windscreen. The two-bladed Hartzell propellor is usually placed in horizontal position when the aircraft is on the ground. Because the engine runs at constant speed, the speed of the aircraft is controlled by the throttle which is fitted with a governor that controls the pitch of the propellor.

Below: Notice the white GPS antenna and the two hoisting points on either side of it.

Photo: Robert Pied

Photo: Robert Pied

Photo: Robert Pied

Photo: Robert Pied

Above: On the starboard side of the aircraft, immediately in front of the windscreen, the Atmospheric Pressure Measuring probe is located. Underneath it is the air intake for the air conditionning system.

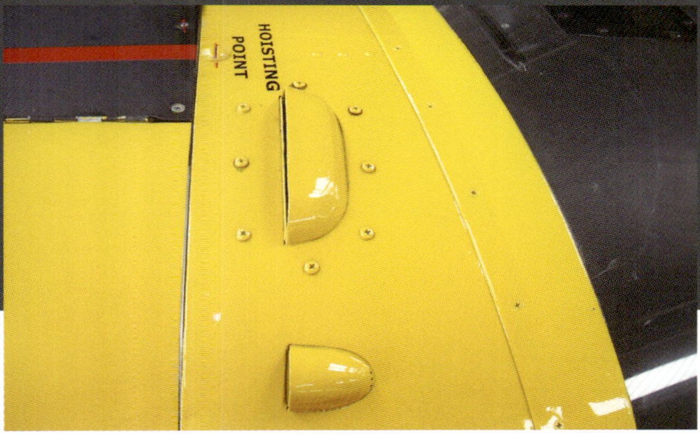

Photo: Robert Pied

Right: A good overall view of the windscreen and the canopy of the SF.260. Notice the Air Temperature Measuring probe central on the windscreen, immediately above of the rear-view mirror. The handle to open the canopy and slide it back is also placed central. The initial SF.260 M had a large, but rather shallow canopy, but these were replaced when the aircraft got updated.

Photo: Robert Pied

Learning to fly

Can you remember the first time you got behind the wheel of a car and the nerves you felt racing through your body? Now imagine adding a dimension to that. Not only can you go left and right, but also up and down. This exciting experience is what makes flying so wonderful, but first, you need to control the aircraft and learn every technical aspect of it. This is the cockpit in which for so many pilots around the world, that adventure began. We get into the cockpit of the SIAI Marchetti SF.260 further on in this book, but these two photos by Giorgio Ciarini get pretty close to capturing that feeling of learning to fly. Especially when you consider that in the photo to the right, 3 aircraft are flying in close formation!

Photo: Giorgio Ciarini

SF-260 Marchetti
Forward fuselage

Photo: Giorgio Ciarini

Photo: Robert Pied

Photo: Robert Pied

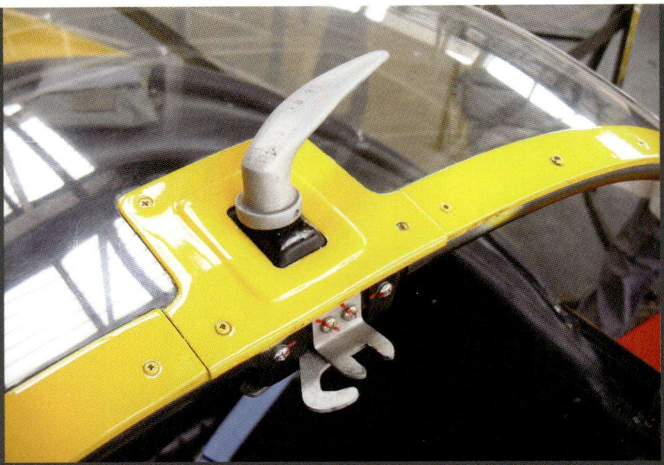

Above: Another view of the handle that opens the canopy. The large canopy slided aft on a pair of rails to the side of the fuselage.
Left: A close-up view of the Air Temperature Measuring probe placed centrally on the windscreen.

Photo: Bart Rosselle

Photo: Robert Pied

Above: A closer look at the Atmospheric Pressure Measuring probe on the starboard side of the fuselage. Better not touch that!
Left: Sr. Captain Collard is at the controls of one of the red painted aircraft of the Demonstration Team 'Red Devils'. Nice watch too, by the way!

Photo: Giorgio Ciarini

Photo: Robert Pied

Photo: Robert Pied

Top: An SF.260 EA is about to go on another training mission. Notice that the central part of the canopy is tinted and the different battery compartement and electrical hook-up of this type.
Above: A good view of the larger and wider bubble canopy which was introduced on the SF.260 D model.

Photo: Robert Pied

Photo: Robert Pied

Above: On either side of the canopy, a handle is located, which allows the pilot and his student to push back the large canopy, in order to get into the aircraft.

Above: This photo shows ST-17 of the Belgian Air Force, a M-model of the Marchetti, before it's upgrade. Of interest is the early type of canopy. Compare it to those on page 21.

Photo: Robert Pied

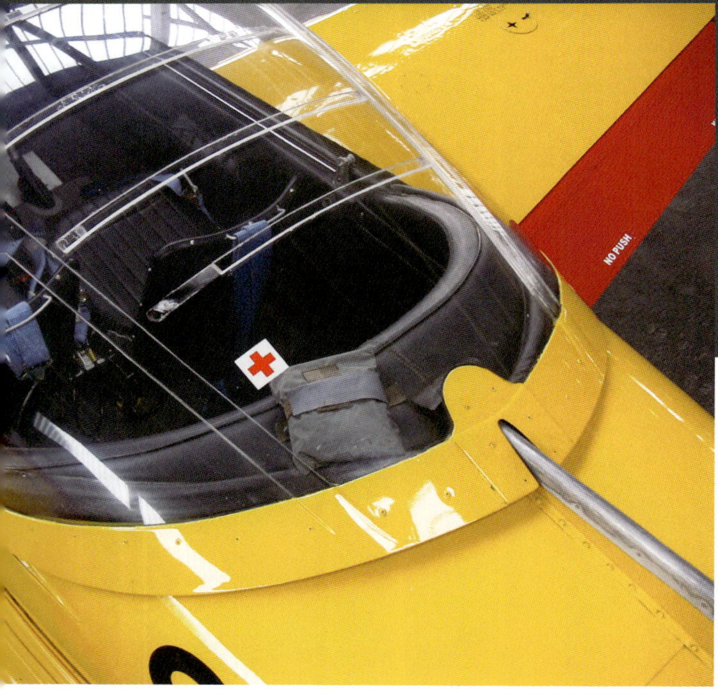

Above and left: These two photos also shows the early style canopy of the SIAI Marchetti SF.260M. Notice the line running over it in the photo to the left. When the Belgian Air Force received the SF.260D in 1992, it was delivered with a larger and wider canopy, offering a much improved view to the crew. Today, all the remaining original M-versions of the aircraft still in use, have been fitted with the new type of canopy. The D-model is slightly heavier than the older M-model and comes in at 1,028 kg when the 4 fuel tanks are full.

Photo: Walter Van Bel

Photo: Robert Pied

Photo: Robert Pied

Right: Compare the blown canopy in this photo with the more flat canopy in the photos on the opposite page, which is the old version. Today all remaining SF.260s of the Belgian Air Force have the newer, higher canopy.

Photo: Giorgio Ciarina

Photo: Walter Van Bel

Above: A pair of Italian SF.260 EAs is flying along the Italian coast during a formation training flight. Notice the difference on the aft part of the fuselage with the other aircraft in this book.

Left: The Italian SF.260 has the central part of the large canopy tinted. Notice the large blade antenna on the base of the vertical tail and the wing fence.

Photo: Augusto Quincke

Photo: Robert Pied

Above: The Marchetti SF.260 proved to be a very successful export product, with over 30 air forces all over the world to use it either as a trainer or as a close support aircraft. The photo above, made by Augusto Quincke, shows one of the 12 SF.260 that were ordered by the Uruguayan Air Force. It sports markings indicating the many hours that the type has flown in the country, training future pilots.

Right: A very clear November morning in 2020 and this SF.260M is about to land at Beauvechain AB. Notice the details of the aircraft's belly, such as the VHF antenna, navigation light and landing gear.

Photo: Walter Van Bel

Photo: Robert Pied

Photo: Robert Pied

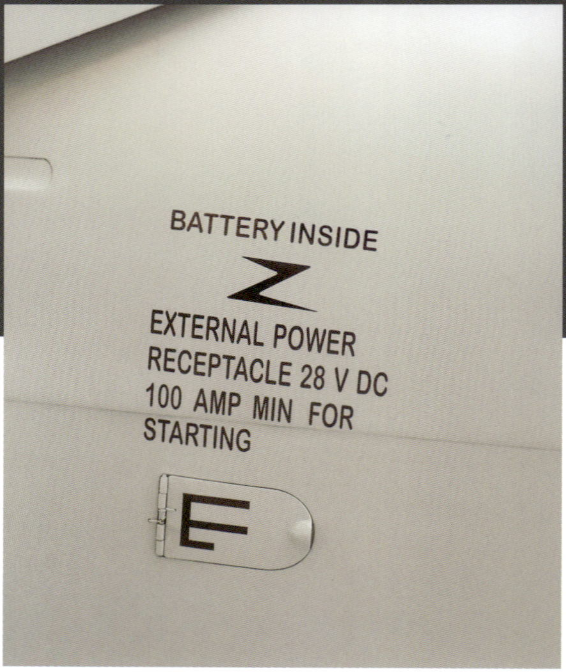

Photo: Robert Pied

Top: In 2019, the Belgian Air Force celebrated the 50th anniversary of the introduction of the type and for this occasion, some aircraft received special markings on the vertical tail. The photos above and right show the three different types of navigation lights, located on the aircraft's belly.

Photo: Giorgio Ciarini

Above: The Italian Air Force, much like the others operating the aircraft, has used the SIAI Marchetti SF.260 extensively. This orange painted trainer sports the impressive achievement of 235,500 flying hours of the type. Notice the large, white painted blade antenna at the base of the tail and the lowered flaps.

Photo: Robert Pied

Photo: Robert Pied

Above and left: One of the external differences between the M and D-version, is the location of the battery compartment on the port side of the fuselage. These photos shows it on the M. On the D-version, it is located more forward, over the wing root.

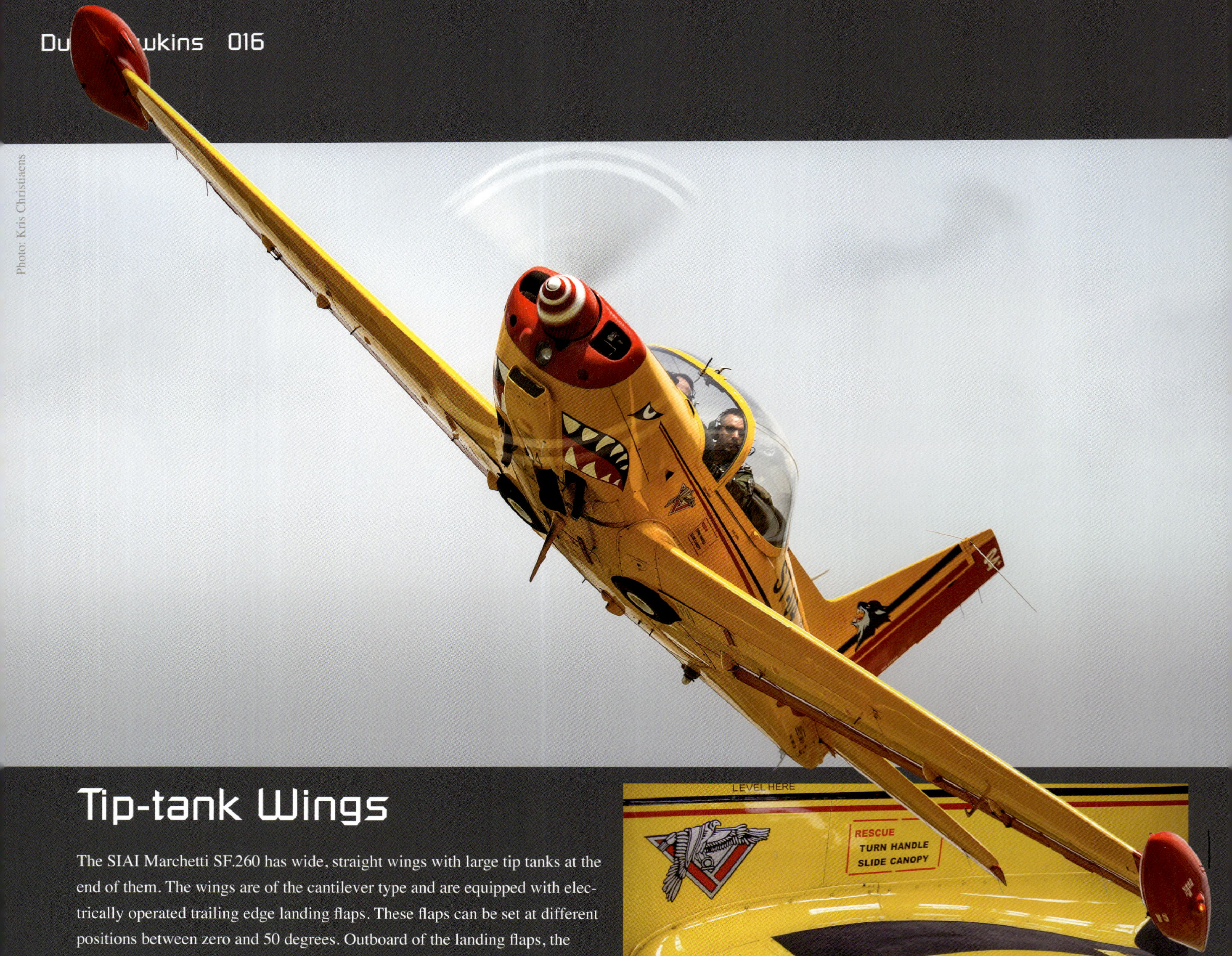

Photo: Kris Christiaens

Tip-tank Wings

The SIAI Marchetti SF.260 has wide, straight wings with large tip tanks at the end of them. The wings are of the cantilever type and are equipped with electrically operated trailing edge landing flaps. These flaps can be set at different positions between zero and 50 degrees. Outboard of the landing flaps, the Ailerons are located, which are each equipped with an aerodynamic trim-tab and a pair of static dischargers.

At the wing root, black material is placed, ensuring that the crew doens't slip when they enter or exit the cockpit. Notice in the photo above that the landing gear wheels aren't covered when the gear is retracted. A pitot tube is located underneath the port, about halfway along.

Photo: Robert Pied

Right: A close-up of the SF.260's wingroot, with the black area where the pilot steps to get into the cockpit.

Photo: Robert Pied

Below: The cover over the aileron actuator on top of the wing in close-up. Notice the position of it in the photo beneath it.

Photo: Robert Pied

Below: 30 degree angle, turning around a fixed spot: that's a 2G turn over the Belgian Air Force base of Beauvechain - notice the runways 04L and 04R. Notice the two static dischargers on the aileron.

Photo: Bart Rosselle

Photo: Giorgio Ciarini

Above: A trio of SIAI Marchetti SF.260 EA of the Italian Air force fly in close formation. Notice the Black and orange tip tanks, as well as the horizontal blade antenna underneath the aft fuselage.

Right: This birds-eye view of the port wing of the SF.260 shows some interesting details, such as the walkways near the fuselage, the wing refuelling point, the hoisting point near the trailing edge flap and the flap itself. Notice the structure of the wing, flap and aileron. In this and other photos it is abundantly clear that the Marchettis of the Belgian Air Force are kept in a near perfect condition and extremely clean.

Photo: Robert Pied

Right: ST-32, an SF.260 M that has been updated, is making a turn to the right. This photo shows the underside of the wings to good effect. Notice the position of the navigation light, slightly to the port side of the fuselage.

Below: Next to the walkway, the inner flap mechanism is covered by a small panel, fixed to the wing with 3 screws.

Photo: Bart Rosselle

Photo: Robert Pied

Photo: Robert Pied

Above: The actuator covers of the trailing edge flap and aileron, underneath the wing seen from below and the front.
Right: The completely lowered trailing edge flap, showing the position of the second hinge, towards the aileron.

Photo: Robert Pied

Photo: Robert Pied

Photo: Robert Pied

Photo: Robert Pied

Photo: Robert Pied

Above & Left: The refueling points on the wings of the SF.260. The aircraft has 4 fuel tanks; one in each wing and the tiptanks. The latter hold 144 litres combined while the wing tanks can each hold 49,5 litres. The D-version has electrical fuel pumps, the M-version has a mechanical pump.

This photo shows a quartet of Marchetti SF.260s of the Belgian Air Force in a formation flight training. Notice the different shapes of the VHF/COMM 1 antennas located on the belly of the aircraft. ST-32 is an SF.260M, with a straight antenna, while ST-47 is an SF.260D with a bent antenna. Or you can just read it of the aft fuselage, underneath the horizontal tails...

Photo: Robert Pied

Photo: Robert Pied

November 2020 and the Covid-19 pandemic is still raging all over the world. No reason to stop training student pilots though, but safety and health have to be kept at all conditions, hence the masks worn by both crew members. ST-03 was one of the first SIAI Marchetti SF.260 M to be delivered to the Belgian Air Force. It entered service in March of 1970 and is the second oldest aircraft in the current fleet - ST-02 is the oldest, while the first one, ST-01 crashed only 18 months after being delivered. This accured during an aerobatic training flight with 4 aircraft, with ST-01 in the number 4 position, losing control during a loop manoeuvre. Unfortunately, the pilot, Adj. Paul Verbeek got killed in the crash.

Photo: Robert Pied

Photo: Robert Pied

One of the recognisable things of the SIAI MArchetti SF.260, are its tip tanks and these photos give you a very close look at them. Each tip tank can hold 72 litres of fuel. These tank are fixed to the wings and can't be jetissoned.

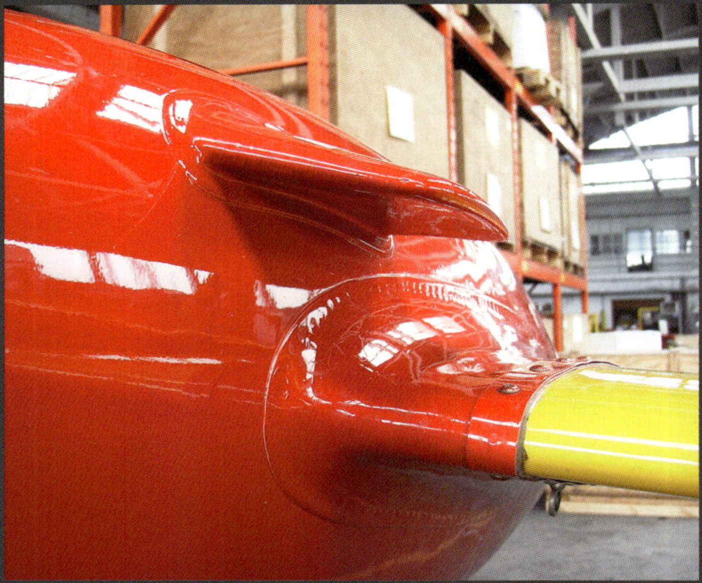

Photo: Robert Pied

Above: To improve aerodynamic flow over the wing, small winglets are located immediately above and in front of the wings. Right: This photo of the underside of the starboard wing near the tip tank shows where the aircraft can be hooked up to be secured to the ground.

Photo: Robert Pied

Photo: Robert Pied

Photo: Robert Pied

Above: At the far end of each wing tip tank, a navigation light is positionned, red on the port side and blue on the starboard side. When doing his walk-around, the pilot checks both the lights to make sure they are clean and ready to function.

Photo: Robert Pied

Above: underneath the wing tip tank - in this case of an Italian Marchetti, a drain is installed. In case of an emergency, the remaining fuel can be dumped by opening this valve.

Photo: Robert Pied

Above and right: The 4 fuel tanks of the SF.260 - two in the wings, two in the tip tanks - all have their own filler cap. The photo above shows it closed; to the right it is opened by turning the two wing nuts.

Photo: Robert Pied

Cockpit close-up

Photo: Kris Christiaens

The cockpit of the SIAI Marchetti SF.260 is where it all begins and happens for the student pilots. The cockpit is very spacious and offers side-by-side seating for the pilots. Behind the two seats - very much like spartan car seats - a bench is installed for a third person. When flying the aircraft, each person carries his/her own parachute on the back. Thanks to the one piece windscreen and the large canopy, all round visibility is excellent, as can be seen in the photo above. In this chapter, we'll take a closer look at the cockpit and everything in it. For this, we show you three different versions of the cockpit: the updated SF.260M, the SF.260D, both of the Belgian Air Force and the SF.260 EA, in service with the Italian Air Force. The photo above shows the cockpit of ST-12, an M-model. It is however the modernised version of the SF.260M. This specific aircraft entered service with the Belgian Air Force in June of 1970, which makes this a very good looking 50 year old aircraft. Notice the dual control sticks and the compass on top of the instrument panel. The pilots are secured in their seits by means of blue four-point seat belts, attached to the back and the sides of the seats.

Photo: Robert Pied

Photo: Laurent Heyligen

Compare the photos on this page to the one on the opposite page; these are of an SF.260D, which is a more modern version of the SF.260. The photo above shows the control stick in close-up. Notice in the photo to the right the airspeed indicator, the large dial to the left.

Photo: Laurent Heyligen

Photo: Robert Pied

Above: Central on the instrument board is the engine check panel with the red emergency canopy release handle next to it.

Photo: Giorgio Ciarini

Cockpit close-up

Thousands of military pilots made their first flights in the SIAI-Marchetti SF-260. In this chapter, we take a closer look at the cockpit of the aircraft. The Marchetti is used to teach the principles of flight to student-pilots, and in the more advanced programs for things like navigation, formation flying, night flying, aerobatics, and so on. There isn't a pilot that doesn't remember his first solo flight in this very capable and forgiving trainer. Let's have a closer look!

Right: This photo gives a good view on the instrument panel of an SF.260 EA, with the airspeed indicator to the left, showing a speed of around 125 knots. To the right of it are the artificial horizon and the altimeter. See where the same instruments are located in front of the pilot on the right side of the panel? Notice the group of 8 small dials in front of the pilot; these indicate the oil and cylinder temperature, oil and fuel pressure on the top row and the quantity of fuel left in each of the 4 fuel tanks in the bottom row. In his left hand, the pilot holds the throttle. Notice the throttle for the left seat. Ow, flashy shoes, Giorgio!

Photo: Giorgio Ciarini

Photo: Robert Pied

Photo: Robert Pied

Left: The central console of an SF.260M. Above: Part of the ventilation and heating system on either side of the compass.

Photo: Robert Pied

Early style cockpit

These photos show the updated cockpit of a SIAI Marchetti SF.260M. It's only a detail, but have a look at the side compartements of this aircraft: they're black and have room for maps. Compare these to the photos of the D version on page 37. Notice the 5 switches below on the left side: the red one on the right is for the Boost Pump, while the other 4 are for the Navigation light, Strobe light, Landing light and Pitot heat. To the left of them the circuit breakers. Notice in the central console the Emergency Landing Gear lever, which is used in case of electrical failure.

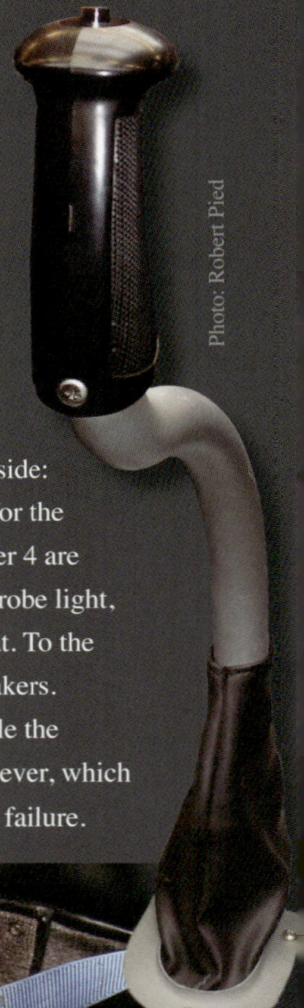

Photo: Robert Pied

Photo: Robert Pied

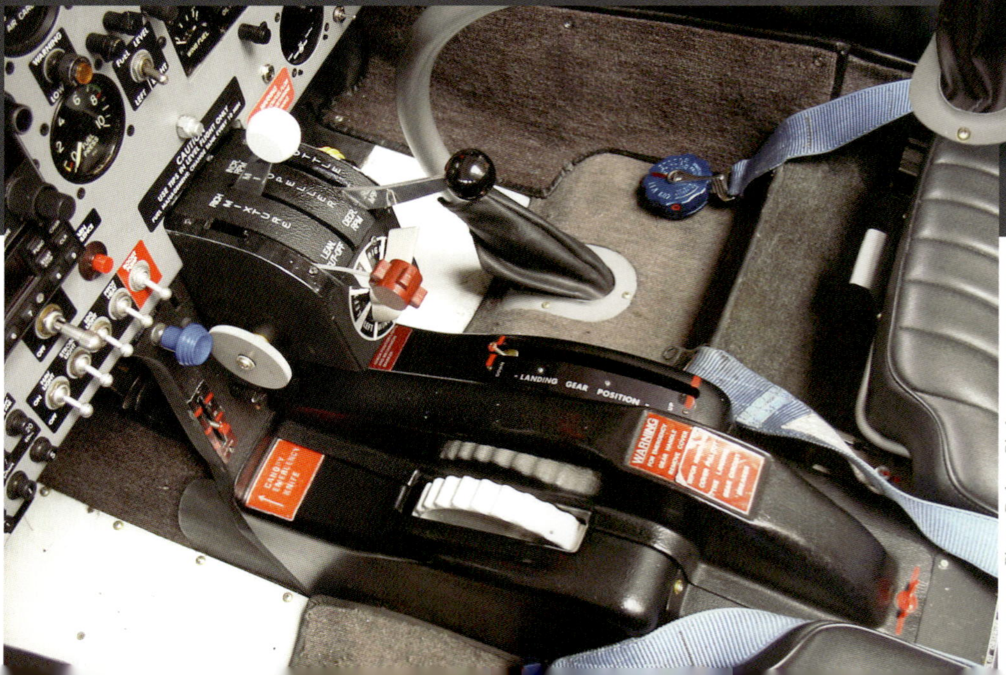

Photo: Robert Pied

SF-260 Marchetti Cockpit

Below: The Compass of ST-17 - an aircraft that was delivered to the Belgian Air Force in September 1970 - placed on top of the instrument panel. Notice the indication of LASAR underneath it - Limited Authority Spark Advance Regulator, which controls the ignition process of the engine.

Photo: Robert Pied

Photo: Robert Pied

Above: The cockpit and instrument panel seen from the starboard side. Notice the Landing Gear switch with the Remove Before Flight tag fixed to it. Notice the dials in the middle of the instrument panels, with the RPM indicator, Fuel flow and Air Speed indicator. To the right are the Artificial Horizon and the Altimeter. Below those, the compass and rate of climb indicator. Notice the position of the radio equipment.

Photo: Robert Pied

Photo: Robert Pied

Left: A closer look at the rudder pedals of the port seat. See the throttle?
Above: the right side of the instrument panel with the panel light switch. In the upper left corner is the start switch. It has 5 positions: Off, Right-hand ignition circuit, Left-hand ignition circuit, Simultanius ignition switch and Start.

Photo: Robert Pied

Photo: Robert Pied

Far left: The rear-view mirror attached to the top of the windscreen.
Below left: This photo shows the seats of the Marchetti and the attachment points of the blue seat belts. Notice how the seats can be moved forward and backwards.
Below: This grey painted SF.260D was photographed whilst being in maintenance. Notice how the instrument panel is lit up for engine checks. Check out the cockpit floor with the seats removed.

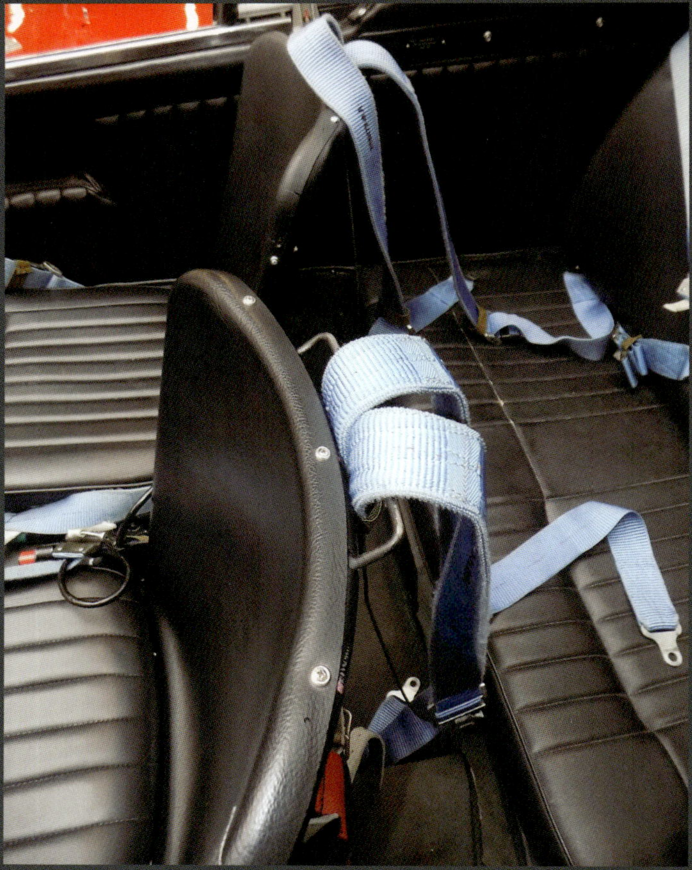

Photo: Robert Pied

Photo: Robert Pied

Photo: Robert Pied

Photo: Robert Pied

Sitting Comfy? These photos show the seats inside the cockpit. To get into the seats, just climb on the wing, turn the handle on top of the canopy and slide it back. You can taxi with the canopy open and even fly with it slightly open, but not faster than 120 knots.The maximum speed of the aircraft is 236 knots.

Photo: Robert Pied

Photo: Robert Pied

Photo: Robert Pied

Above: Some additional photos of the cockpit of the modernised SF.260M. Notice the head phone connections in between the two seats in the photo above. Look at the buttons fixed on the control stick in the photo above right.

Photo: Robert Pied

According to some of the most experienced pilots we spoke, the Marchetti is a very forgiving aircraft, easy to fly, with no specific vices and ideal for teaching students how to fly. One pilot explained that it is a matter of speed or altitude: if you want to go low, you need to add speed to your manoeuvres. When you get higher, slower manoeuvres can be done, like stalls.

Photo: Giorgio Ciarini

Above: Another photo of ST-46, a SIAI Marchetti SF.260D with the instrument panel lit up. In front of it are a large number of aircraft with a variety of liveries, in various state of maintenance.

Photo: Giorgio Ciarini

Above and right: Giorgio Ciarini sent us these two interesting photos of a flight simulator that is being used to train student pilots in various situations. Notice in the photo above how realistic the view is! The photo to the right shows that the simulator is almost the entire aircraft! just wings and tail are mission, but it even has a landing gear!

Photo: Bart Rosselle

Red Devils

Belgian Air Force Demo Team

Photo: Bart Rosselle

Above: Perfect formation, despite the grim weather that can be typical of Belgian early spring. The Belgian Air Force Demo Team "Red Devils" was created in 1957 - although it adopted the name officially in 1959 - then flying the Hawker Hunter. After the retirement of the Hunters, the team continued flying demonstrations on the French Fouga Magister jet trainer from 1965 to 1977. The SIAI Marchetti SF.260 however proved to be a perfect airplane for aerobatics too and in 1973, Sr. Cpt. Frank Fonderie and ADC Karel Serrien formed a demo team called "The Swallows", which continued to fly until 1981. In 2011, the "Red Devils" were brought back to life and a 4-ship of SF.260 began flying displays during the airshow season in Belgium and the surrounding countries. Some 10 years later, they continue to do so.

Photo: Bart Rosselle

When they aren't performing, the aircraft of the Red Devils are used for pilot training. Must be pretty cool to fly in one of those red painted SF.260s. Notice the horizontal position of the Hartzell constant speed propeller. The Lycoming engine runs at a constant speed - a governor on the throttle controls the pitch of the propeller.

Photo: Bart Rosselle

Photo: Bart Rosselle

Above: The nose of a Red Devil Marchetti SF.260 and its menacing shark mouth. These aircraft are always kept in a very clean condition. Notice the 2014-18 marking, in commemoration of the centenary of the First World War.

Right: Tight formation, turning to starboard. Notice that the wheels of the tricycle landing gear remain visible when retracted.

Below: The Belgian Air Force Red Devils get into formation for the camera. The little trainer has proven to be an excellent aircraft for aerobatics - quite a few of the aircraft have been bought by private pilots, enjoying the forgiving nature of it.

Photo: Bart Rosselle

Right: ST-31 is waiting for another training flight on the tarmac at Beauvechain Air Base in Belgium. The SIAI Marchetti SF.260 has a wing span of 8,35 meter and a length of 7,10 meter. As mentionned before, it is an agile little trainer and has a 6G / -3G limit during manoeuvres, which is quite a lot for such a small airplane. Especially when you consider that you can't rely on a G-suit when flying it!

Photo: Peter Anthoni

Photo: Walter Van Bel

Above: 2019 and the Red Devils are preparing to take off from Kleine Brogel Air Base for a demo flight. The 4 aircraft received a special paint on the vertical to commemorate the 50th anniversary of the type entering service with the Belgian Air Force.

Below: Red Devil ST-34 is being checked and about to be refuelled for another training. The engine runs on ordinary petrol and it takes a while to fill up the 4 fuel tanks in the wings and tip tanks. When flying at it's most economic regime, the aircraft has a range of just over 2,000 km.

Photo: Peter Anthoni

Photo: Laurent Heyligen

Landing the Marchetti

Time to get a closer look at the Marchetti's landing gear. The landing gear is a typical tricycle landing gear, with a nosewheel and a tire for each of the gears. The forward gear simply folds back, while the main gear fold inwards. The photo above shows a Belgian Air Force SF-260D - actually the last to be delivered in June of 1992 - in approach to Kleine Brogel AB during the 2009 Tiger Meet, hence the livery applied for the occasion.

Right: The mechanism of the front landing gear of the Marchetti, with the forked strut pulling back the gear aft into the wheel well. Notice the metal coloured tubing inside the forward part of the bay.

Photo: Robert Pied

Photo: Robert Pied

Photo: Robert Pied

Photo: Robert Pied

The nose landing gear is located underneath the engine and in between the two engine exhausts. Notice in the photo above the connection to the sole landing gear door, which is painted white on the inside. The photo to the right shows a towing bar connected to the rim of the nose wheel.

Photo: Robert Pied

Photo: Robert Pied

Left: For this photo, Robert was on the ground, looking up - he had a bad back that day, so this photo shows his commitment to this book! Look at the position of the two engine exhausts, on either side of the wheel and the earthing point on the starboard side of the aircraft. When the landing gear is retracted, it fold aft into the gear bay, but the wheel itself remains visible in flight.

Below left: This Turkish Marchetti is painted white with a black anti glare part on top of the engine cover. The landing gear of the aircraft is always painted white.

Below: This photo shows the nose landing gear connected to it's framing, with all engine panels removed.

Photo: Gert Trachez

Photo: Robert Pied

Right: A look inside the nose landing gear bay. Notice where the wheel goes and the cylinder to stop it smoothly. Halfway into the bay is the metal coloured strut pulling the gear inwards. In the photo below, you can see where it is connected to the gear itself. Look how close it is to the engine and the exhausts.

Below right: The Y-shaped aft strut and the connection to the fuselage, seen from below and the front.

Photo: Robert Pied

Photo: Robert Pied

Photo: Jean-Paul Vingerhoed

Photo: Laurent Heyligen

Photo: Robert Pied

Photo: Robert Pied

The landing gear of the SIAI Marchetti SF.260 is a straightforward tricycle gear which is operated electrically, with to each of the gears one landing gear door attached. These do however not cover the wheels.

Left: These photos show the main gear wheels, from the inside. Notice the connection and the brake system, as well as the connection to the landing gear door. The main wheels are pulled inwards when the gear is retracted. Notice the structure of the main gear bay.

Photo: Robert Pied

Above: The link between the landing gear door and the strut, seen from the front of the aircraft. Looks like there was a little bit of overspray when the aircraft was in the paintshop...

Photo: Robert Pied

Photo: Robert Pied

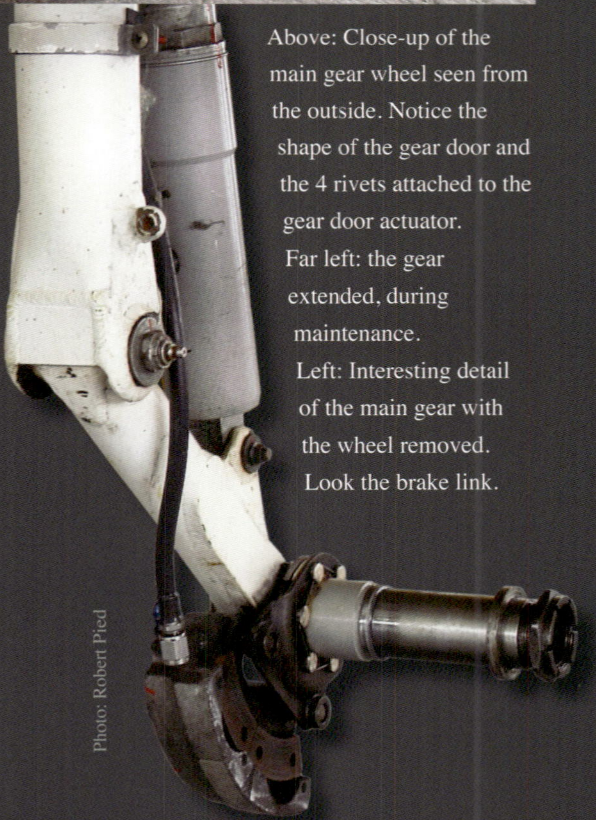

Photo: Robert Pied

Above: Close-up of the main gear wheel seen from the outside. Notice the shape of the gear door and the 4 rivets attached to the gear door actuator.

Far left: the gear extended, during maintenance.

Left: Interesting detail of the main gear with the wheel removed. Look the brake link.

Photo: Bart Rosselle

Photo:Robert Pied

Above: This head-on view of one of the 'Red Devils' of the Belgian Air Force shows the tricycle landing gear and the way the aircraft 'sits' on the ground. The pilot has already lowered the flaps of his aircraft somewhat. When the landing gear is down and locked, the nose gear is connected to the foot pedals, so that the pilot can stear the aircraft on the ground. Once the aircraft is in the air and the pilot retracts the gear, the nose gear automatically disconnects from the foot pedals. While retracting or lowering the gear - by means of the red lever on the instrument panel, see page 36, 37 and on - the pilot hears a signal until the gear is either fully up or locked down.
Left: This photo shows the port main landing gear bay. Look at the spring on the inside of the bay and the actuator for the gear strut.

Right: This photo shows the detached wing of an SF.260 while being in deep maintenance. It does however show to good effect how the gear is folded into the gear bay and the wires running through the bay. Notice the green-yellow primer on the entire part.

Photo:Robert Pied

Photo:Robert Pied

Photo:Robert Pied

Above: The main gear door seen from the front.
Right: A wide angle shot of the port main landing gear of one of the 'Red Devils'. Notice the openings in the gear bay and the actuator.

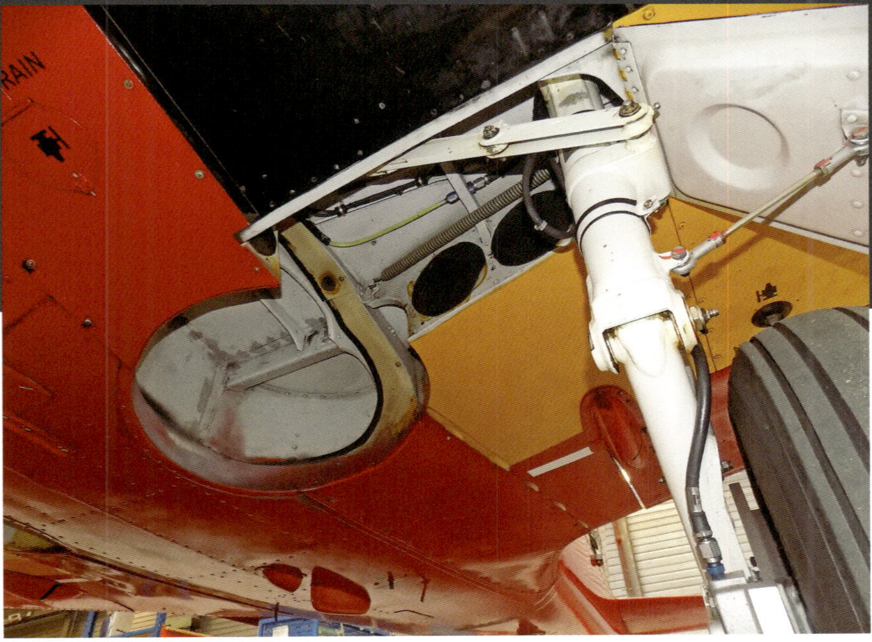

Photo:Robert Pied

Photo: Rogier Westerhuis

Marchetti SF.260 TP

Photo: Rogier Westerhuis

In 1980, a new version of the SIAI Marchetti SF.260 was introduced: the SF.260TP. This variant was powered with an Allison 250-B17D Turboprop engine, which produces up to 420 hp during take off. To this larger engine, the entire nose of the aircraft had to be redesigned. Another new feature of the TP-version, is the three-bladed propeller with a newly designed spinner. The SF.260TP has underwing pylons for weapons; this version can be used as a close air support aircraft, as can be seen in these photos made by Rogier Westerhuis of Philippine Air Force's Marchettis. Notice the longer nose and extended exhausts.

Photo: Rogier Westerhuis

Photo: Rogier Westerhuis

The Philippine Air Force operates different versions of the SF.260. Back in the 1970s, it ordered 32 SF.260M for pilot traing and 16 SF.260W - Warrior. The latter have been disarmed in the 1980s to join the M-version in the pilot training role. Of the TP-version, 18 were ordered, of which the first was delivered in 1993. These photos show the armed SF.260TP. Notice the underwing pylons, fixed on the leading edge of the wing. Of interest are also the large whip-antenna on the port side of the vertical tail extension, aft of the canopy and the white blade antenna next to it. See in the photo above how the shark-mouths differ. Notice the Head-Up Display - HUD - in front of the starboard seat and the white markings on the wings.

Photo: Rogier Westerhuis

Left: This photo shows an SF-260W of the Philippine Air Force, after it was modified to the pilot training role. Six of these aircraft were sold in 1986 to Burkina Faso. Notice the partically tinted canopy.

Below: Another customer for the SIAI Marchetti SF.260TP was the Sri Lanka Air Force, which had 21 of the type in its fleet. Today, they are all retired. Again, notice the longer, sleeker nose of the Allison 250-B17D-engined aircraft. Notice the smaller antennas near the base of the vertical tail.

Photo: Rogier Westerhuis

SF-260 Marchetti TP

Photo: Rogier Westerhuis

Photo: Rogier Westerhuis

Above: A Sri Lankan SF.260TP is patrolling the seas around the island and the ships navigating them. Looks to me like the Queen of the Netherlands, a suction hopper dredger ship with a length of some 230 m. could use some paint...

Right: A good view of the profile of a very clean Sri Lanka Air Force SF.260TP. Notice that it has an additional underwing pylon and that the propeller blades are in feathered position. See the extended exhausts?

Photo: Giorgio Ciarini

Photo: Robert Pied

Time to take a closer look at the vertical tail of the SIAI Marchetti SF.260. The tail has a long, near horizontal base, starting immediately aft of the cockpit. The fin itself has a large rudder which is about half of the entire surface of the vertical tail. Near the top, a pair of static dischargers is placed. In front of the tail, communication and navigation equipment is located. Above: the vertical of some SF.260 EAs of the Italian Air force.

There are some small difference to be found on the different versions of the Marchetti, like the communication antennas; some have a blade antenna at the base, others have smaller VHF/COMM2 and GPS antenna's placed on it, but the basic shape of all the aircraft are the same.

Right: A Turkish Marchetti is making a pass against a clear blue sky. Turkey ordered 40 of the type back in 1990. The first six of the order were built in Italy, but the remaining 34 were built under licence in Turkey by Turkish Aerospace Industries. They are used for basic pilot training at the 123rd Training Squadron, based at Izmir, near the Aegean Sea. Notice the engine exhausts stains clearly visible against the white painted belly of the aircraft.

Photo: Gert Trachez

Photo: Giorgio Ciarini

Photo: Robert Pied

Photo: Peter Anthoni

Above: A close-up of the VOR/ILS/GS antenna on the leading edge of the vertical tail. VOR stands for Visual Omni Range; the Navigation system of the aircraft also picks up Glideslope Signals, making it possible to do an instrument approach when weather conditions are bad.

Above: The vertical tail of Marchetti ST-40, which received a special medium grey livery when the type celebrated it's 40th anniversary in the Belgian Air Force. Below left: The VHF/ COMM2 antenna near the base of the fin. The VHF/COMM1 antenna is located on the belly of the aircraft.

Photo: Robert Pied

Photo: Robert Pied

Photo: Giorgio Ciarini

Above: A neat line-up of Italian Marchettis. Notice the different inspection panels on the fuselage. Below: The static dischargers on the rudder's trailing edge. Additional pairs can be found on each of the ailerons and the horizontal tails.

Photo: Robert Pied

Above: The VOR/ILS/GS antenna seen from above. Notice how far the white antennas extend. The SF.260 proved to be a reliable aircraft for the Belgian Air Force, with the last one written off during a ground accident over 20 years ago, in October 2000.

Photo: Robert Pied

Photo: Robert Pied

The horizontal tail and aft fuselage of the Marchetti in all it's details. When on the ground, the aircraft's elevators are always lowered, as can be seen in these photos.

Photo: Robert Pied

Above: The area underneath the horizontal tails where the serial number of the aircraft is indicated. Notice another point where the aircraft can be hooked to the ground - the other points are near the wingtips

Photo: Robert P

Photo: Robert Pied

Photo: Robert Pied

Above and right: At the far end of the fuselage, a navigation light is positionned. Look at the elevator's extensions fixed on the aft fuselage and the rivets of the elevators themselves.

Photo: Robert Pied

Photo: Robert Pied

Above: The hinging point for the elevator on the horizontal tails. An interesting detail for the scale modellers among you!

Left: The port aft fuselage, looking aft, with the wing to horizontal tail joint.

Maintaining the Marchetti

The SIAI Marchetti SF.260 not only has had a long career, during it's career, it has been flown extensively. Each student pilot has to fly many hours on it to get familiar with the basics of flying, before being transferred to another type. This also means that the aircraft have to be maintained constantly and for this, highly trained engineers and mechanics are necessary. This chapter not only shows the SF.260 in maintenance, but it is also a tribute to the skilled crews making sure that the aircraft remain in prestine condition. The photo on the opposite page shows a team of technicians checking an Italian Marchetti, from the engine to the cockpit and the flight controls. The aircraft has been placed on jacks and a cradle and has the engine panels and propeller removed. We'll get a much closer look at the area in the next few pages. With the canopy removed, the technicians have easier access to all equipment in the cockpit. Notice that the trailing edge flaps are removed as well as the wing-fuselage connection.

Photo: Robert Pied

Right: This Belgian SF.260 has it's engine removed, as well as many parts that are attached to the engine firewall. Notice the tubing to which the engine is attached. In the maintenance hangar at Beauvechain air base in Belgium, the aircraft are almost completely taken apart during deep maintenance, it is actually quite impressive. Fortunately, we were able to make loads of photographs... Notice how the retracting strut of the nose landing gear is attached.

Photo: Robert Pied

Photo: Laurent Heyligen

Photo: Robert Pied

Some close-ups of the framing, engine and both connected on this page. Notice the disc in front of the engine in the photo below, where the propellor and spinner fit.

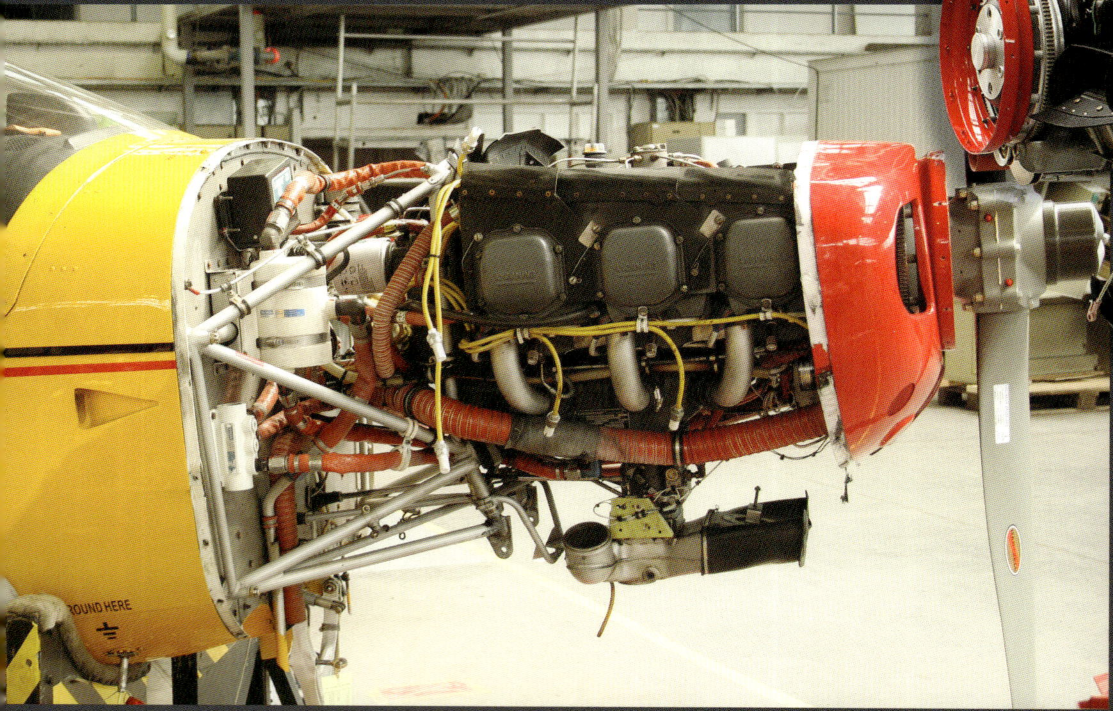

Photo: Laurent Heyligen

Photo: Laurent Heyligen

Photo: Guillaume Friart

Photo: Robert Pied

Photo: Robert Pied

Above: The engine is installed, but the engine exhausts still have to be placed. The engine is checked every 50 hours, during the Intermediate maintenance, but a more thorough inspection is done every 100 hours.

Photo: Duke Archives

The SIAI Marchetti SF.260's engine - the Avco Lycoming AE10-540-D4A5 for the D-version - delivers 260 hp, has six cylinders in line and is air cooled. Since 2003, the Marchettis of the Belgian Air Force received an upgrade when LASAR was installed - Limited Authority Spark Advance Regulator, ensuring a optimised ignition process. Notice the exhaust in the photo below.

Photo: Robert

Photo: Duke Archives

Photo: Duke Archives

SF-260 Marchetti Maintenance

Photo: Duke Archives

Left: This photo shows the proximity of the engine, the air filter underneath it and the nose landing gear of the aircraft. Notice the framing fixed to the firewall and how the engine is hook up to it. In this photo the engine exhausts are not yet fixed. Below: the orange tubing shows how air is directed underneath the engine.

Photo: Duke Archives

Photo: Duke Archives

Photo: Duke Archives

Above: A top view of the Avco Lycoming engine, with all the wiring and connections.

Left: A closer look at the equipment fixed to the firewall of the aircraft, Notice the air intake aft of it.

Photo: Duke Archives

Photo: Duke Archives

Photo: Duke Archives

Above: The engine in the process of being placed to the airframe after deep maintenance. The aircraft undergoes a deep maintenance every 1,500 hours or every 5 years. In this case, nearly every element of the aircraft is taken apart: the entire airframe is inspected, all flying instruments are checked, as well as the communication and navigation equipment, the fuel system and the entire engine. Deep maintenance means that the aircraft is in the maintenance hangar for some 8 months and that all paint is stripped and the aircraft completely repainted inside and out.

The photos below show the same Marchetti as on the opposite page, with the engine parts being placed one by one. Notice the air filter underneath the engine and the engine exhausts that still have to be placed. To make sure that the engine cylinders don't give a problem in extensive use, they are replaced every 1,000 hours. Considering that these aircraft all have had a service of over 50 years, they are in prestine condition, as can be seen in these photos.

Right: This Marchetti SF.260 is almost ready to go back to the flight line. The engine is installed, as are the propellor, engine exhausts and the spinner. Next, the engine panels will be placed and fixed, and after that the aircraft is lowered from it's cradle and an inspection flight is planned.

Photo: Robert Pied

Photo: Duke Archives

Photo: Duke Archives

Photo: Duke Archives

These photos show the same aircraft as the ones on the previous pages - the windscreen is still masked for painting. Almost all of the interior is still missing - with the instrument panel removed, many details can be seen. Much of the electrical wiring can be seen in large bundels aft of the engine firewall, Notice the orange tubing for the airco system and the mechanics of the throttle, connected to the central console. This photo also provides a good view of the rudder pedals and links into the cockpit floor.

The Belgian Air Force Marchettis are all based at Beauvechain Air Base, where they have been since 1996, after the Elementary Flying School moved there from Goetsenhoven Air Base. Today, the aircraft share the base with the NH-90 TTH - Tactical Transport Helicopter - and Agusta A-109 helicopters. The yellow, red or grey SF.160s all carry a wolf's head on the vertical tail, the unit marking of the 1st Training Wing of the Belgian Air Force. Since the aircraft has been delivered, some 3,500 pilots have been trained in Belgium on the SIAI Marchetti SF.260 and it's career is far from being over.

Right: A close-up of the cockpit floor with central part in detail. Notice the sidewalls of the cockpit.

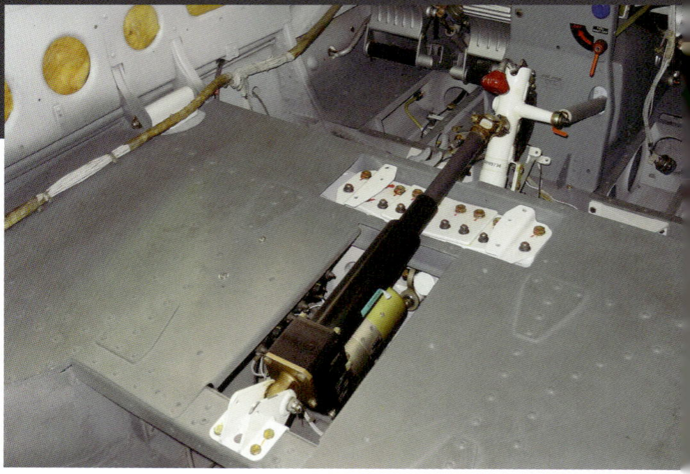

Photo: Duke Archi

Photo: Duke Archives

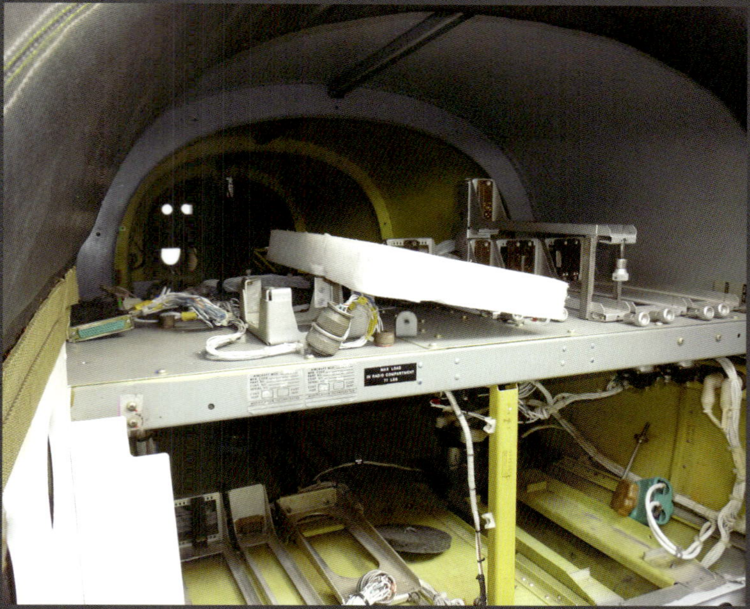

Photo: Duke Archives

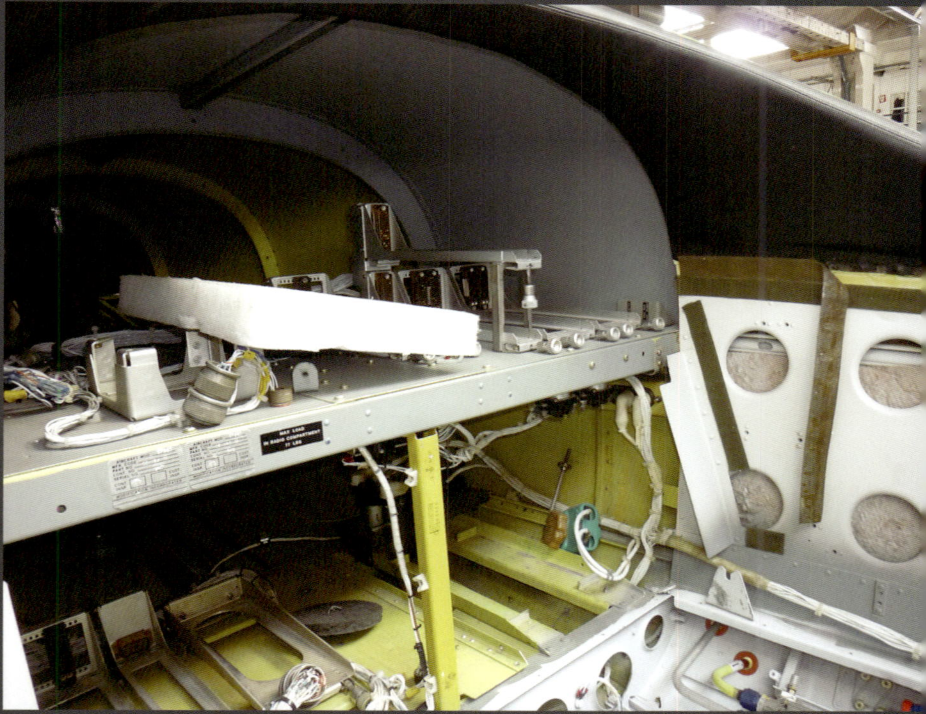

Above and right: The area behind the cockpit seen from the inside; Notice the structure of the airframe and where the aircraft's battery is placed, on the port side of the aircraft.

Photo: Duke Archives

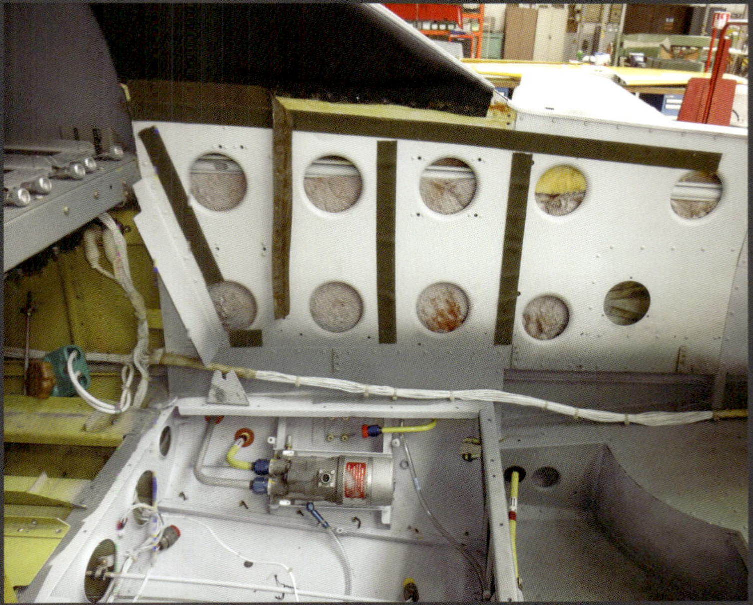

Above: The cockpit floor is removed, showing the structure of the airframe and the wiring running over the floor.

Photo: Duke Archives

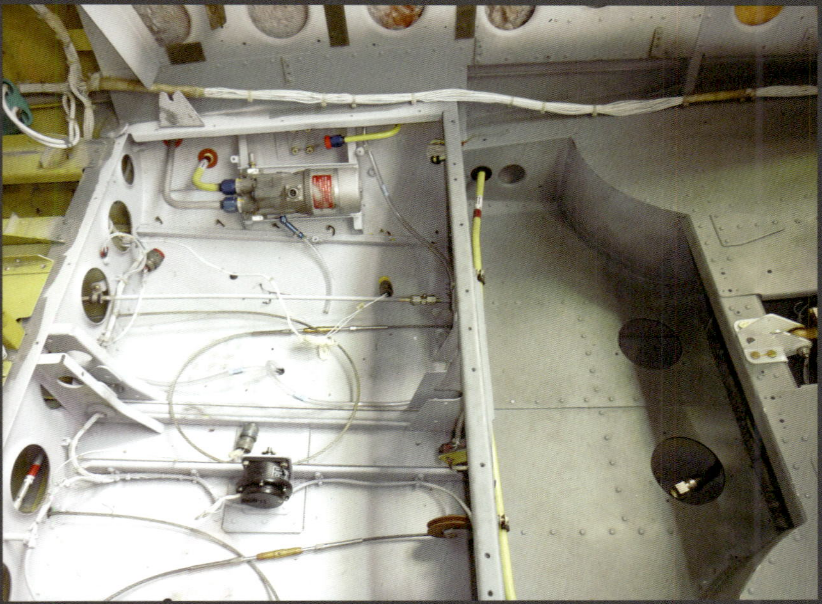

Above: This photo shows the area a little more forward. With the cockpit floor removed, you can see where the landing gear bays are positionned.

Photo: Laurent Heyligen

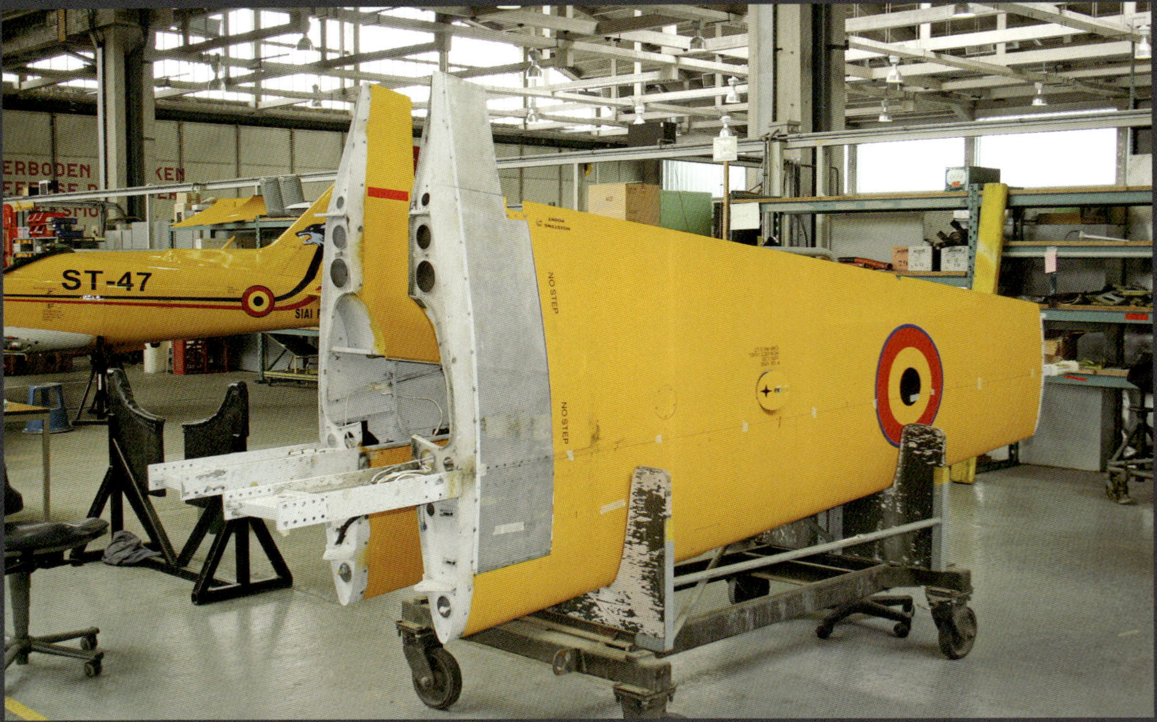

Left: A pair of wings, with the wingtip tanks removed are placed in a special cradle, ready to go into deep maintenance. Notice that the special material of the walkways on the wing root is already removed, as is the landing gear.
Below: The propellor head, waiting for the spinner to be installed.

Photo: Robert Pied

Photo: Peter Anthoni

These photos show some SIAI Marchetti SF.260s in various state of maintenance. the grey one on the opposite page is hooked up to electricity to check some of the engine readings, while the 'Red Devil' below still has a long way to go before it can get back into the air. Notice it's spinner and front engine cover on the racks behind it. ST-47 was one of the final Marchettis to be delivered to the Belgian Air Force in June of 1970. Of the 48 aircraft delivered, 13 were lost in accidents, resulting in the death of 5 pilots.

Photo: Laurent Heyligen

Photo: Robert Pied

Photo: Laurent Heyligen

Photo: Robert Pied

Above: The lower engine cover with it's distinctive shark mouth. The photo above left shows the same engine panel, seen from the inside. Notice the staining of the engine exhausts and the fixed nose wheel door.

Photo: Robert Pied

Above: How is this for a diorama? Maintenance crew have taken out the seats and the cockpit floor of this Marchetti and placed the latter on the wing. The aircraft is placed on jacks and work is being carried out on the engine. Parts of the aft fuselage have been removed as well, as can be seen in the photos below and to the right. Notice the connections to the rudder and elevators in the photos below and right.

Photo: Robert Pied

SF-260 Marchetti Maintenance

Photo: Peter Anthoni

Left: The battery compartment and external power attachment point are visible in this photo, while the complete vertical tail, including it's base are removed. ST-18 has just received it's new wide canopy - the framing is still in primer!

Below left: The aircraft's battery - an M-model - installed, but yet to be connected. This compartment is furter forward on the D-model.

Photo: Robert Pied

Photo: Robert Pied

Photo: Rogier Westerhuis

Above: Just one more photo of the SF.260TP of the Sri lanka Air Force, taken by Rogier Westerhuis. The long nose seems to make the aircraft even more elegant. Notice that the seat in the back is omitted in this version and that it has 4 underwing pylons. Look at the root of the wing's trailing edge flap. It looks like there's a little dent in the top part of the rudder ...

Right: Libya was one of the most important customers of the SF.260, with some 240 ordered back in the 1970s. Some of these found their way to other air forces though... This photo was taken in 2009 by Rob Schleiffert.

Photo: Rob Schleiffert

Photo: Rob Palmer

Left and below: Rob Palmer was able to make these photos of Turkish SF.260s when visiting the country some years ago. Notice that these aircraft, like the Italian SF.260 EAs have the central part of the canopy tinted. Of interest is that the inner parts of the tiptanks are painted black, while the outer parts are orange.

Photo: Rob Palmer

Below: A neat line up of 7 yellow SIAI MArchetti SF.260s seen at their home base of Beauvechain. Notice the remove before flight tags on the underwing pitot tube and a fire extinguisher next to each of the aircraft. All the propellors have been placed in horizontal position.

Photo: Gert Trachez

Photo: Robert Pied

Photo: Robert Pied

Learning to fly

November 2020 and pilot training continues, despite the Covid-19 pandemic raging all over the world. Before the flight crews arrive, ground personnel assures that that the aircraft are in perfect flying condition and fully fuelled-up. I'm not sure what the guy lying on the wing in the photo to the left is doing, but I'm sure he's got a plan! In the photo above, the engine gets a final check, while the canopy is already pulled back and the seat belts out of the cockpit. It's 9 o'clock in the morning and the pilot and his student are in the briefing room, going over the lesson of the day.

Photo: Robert Pied

It takes a while to get the SF.260 fuelled up. Each of the 4 fuel tanks have to be filled individually. No reason to lose your good mood by, though - the ground crew man seems to be happy doing his job! The SIAI Marchetti uses ordinary petrol, in contrast to the jet fuel or kerosine that is used in most military aircraft.

Photo: Robert Pied

Photo: Robert Pied

With the instructor and the student pilot arriving on the flight line, things get serious, especially for the student. Getting into the cockpit is easy enough and while they strap in, the silence reveils the concentration of the duo. While they go over a series of checks, the ground crew man removed the chocks. The fuel lid still has to be closed, though. After a while, the engine is started and while engine and oil temperature is getting up, final checks are being done inside the cockpit. Almost ready to taxi towards the runway!

Of the 125 flying hours that each student has to go through, 41 hours he or she is flying solo. Whenever an instructor thinks that a student needs additional hours of practice, these are granted before the latter can continue his training. When the entire training is completed with good result, he receives his wings and advances to fighter jets, transport aircraft of helicopters. Guess what most hope for...

Photo: Robert Pied

Photo: Robert Pied

Photo: Robert Pied

With the engine at the right temperature, the Marchetti is cleared for taxiing towards the runway. Moments later, the nosewheel is steered towards the runway. It's November, so the canopy is quickly closed. The engine runs, heart rates go up and the ground crew points the right way. The student and his instructor are ready for another training in basic flying, navigation, instrument or formation flying, all aspects that need to be fully mastered before advancing.

Photo: Robert Pied

Photo: Giorgio Ciarini

Photo: Giorgio Ciarini

Above: A trio of Italian SIA Marchetti SF.260 EA is flying in close formation. Notice L-shaped VHF/COMM1 antenna on the belly of the aircraft. Behind it are the TACAN, ADF and navigation light.

Right: One of the Marchettis is taxiing back to his parking spot after a training flight. The landing light is still on. Notice the helmets!

Photo: Bart Rosselle

Photo: Robert Pied

Above: Belgian Air Force's official photographer Bart Rosselle pictured the 'Red Devils' late in the afternoon, flying in perfect formation over the Belgian countryside. What a great shot!

Left: A pilot sitting in a 'Red Devils' Marchetti is saying hi to Robert, before taxiing towards the runway. An experienced pilot, having flown many hours on the E-3A AWACS, he is keeping his flying skills sharp in these strange Covid-19 times. Notice the landing light and the early style VHF antenna on the belly of this SF.260M.

Photo: Erik Gjørup Kristensen

Because of the forgiving nature and the easy handling, many SF.260s found their way into private hands, such as these examples. Marchettis OY-SMA and OY-SMM nowadays fly in Denmark in the colours of Aircombat Europe. Sometimes equipped with a home-made HUD, private pilots can get a feeling of what it is to be a fighter pilot. Like with their military cousins, things aren't always without danger, The aircraft above crashed in 2012, the SF.260 on the right had its canopy detached in flight. Bringing the aircraft safely back to the ground must have been quite an experience.

It was a real pleasure to assemble this 92-page portrait of the elegant SIAI-Marchetti SF.260. I hope you enjoyed going through the pages. Duke

Photo: Erik Gjørup Kristensen